UNIVERSITY OF OXFORD
ASHMOLEAN MUSEUM

THE ANCIENT ROMANS

by

MICHAEL VICKERS

ASHMOLEAN MUSEUM, OXFORD
1992

ASHMOLEAN MUSEUM PUBLICATIONS
Archaeology, History and Classical Studies

Treasures of the Ashmolean
Ancient Cyprus
Ancient Italy
The Arundel Marbles
Greek Vases
Scythian Treasures in Oxford
From Silver to Ceramic
Eat, Drink and Be Merry

UNIFORM WITH THIS VOLUME

Ancient Egypt
The Ancient Near East
Ancient Greek Terracottas

British Library Cataloguing in Publication Data

Vickers, Michael

Ancient Romans
I. Title
936

ISBN 1-85444-026-8

Cover illustration: Detail from G.P. Panini's *A Roman Capriccio*

Designed and typeset by Andrew Ivett
Printed and bound in Singapore by Stamford Press Pte, 1992

Preface

This booklet illustrates life in Rome and its empire with the aid of the material now in the Ashmolean Museum at Oxford. It deals with Italy and the Mediterranean basin, as well as Europe north of the Alps including Britain, during the period between the first century BC and the end of the fourth century AD. There developed in this part of the world a civilization which rivalled and even surpassed those of the ancient Near East; a civilization, moreover, which created many of the social, aesthetic and even physical structures familiar to us today. The language of the Romans was Latin, and a rich original literature has survived. It was also the language of the law and of the church, indeed of learning in general until quite recent times. Kings and emperors regarded imperial Rome as a model of empire, while democrats looked to republican Rome for examples of civic virtue. Today, the tendency for Europe East and West to come together inevitably generates interest in a time when much of Europe was united for centuries.

The Roman collections in the Ashmolean are varied in character. They comprise in the main large-scale marble statues, fresco fragments, coins, articles of bronze, and many vessels of pottery and glass; in other words, objects which it was for the most part unprofitable to recycle in the centuries before they became "collectibles". "Recycling" may be a modish word today, but there is nothing at all new in the concept. Men and women have constantly remade and re-used materials of all kinds. Those which the ancients — and most other people — would have regarded as precious — gold and silver plate, jewellery and gems, exotic woods and textiles — do not figure in any quantity in the archaeological record, having either been melted down and reworked, or having simply perished. What we get in museums is therefore a somewhat haphazard selection of material dependent upon the accident of survival, rather than a true cross-section of what existed in the past. It is the task of the archaeologist to use what has survived together with accounts the Romans have left us of their own world, as aids to the reconstruction of antiquity.

The text of this booklet owes much to previous curators of the Ashmolean's Roman collection, and especially to David Brown now of Oxbow Books. Thanks are due to Ralph Jackson of the British Museum for advice concerning Roman *materia medica,* and to Nick Griffiths for the drawing at Fig. 58. The other drawings were prepared in the Department of Antiquities' Drawing Office by Keith Bennett. Many of the photographs were taken specially for this publication, and most are the work of Michael Dudley and Nick Pollard, to whom go many thanks. Kalinka Huber and Arthur MacGregor were kind enough to read through earlier drafts, and their comments have proved to be extremely useful. The author is, however, responsible for any remaining infelicities or errors.

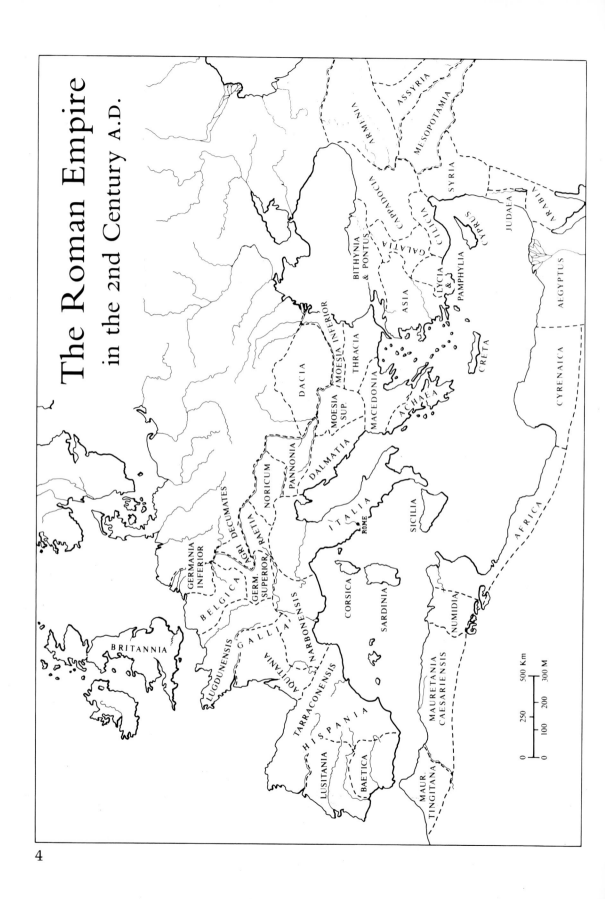

The Roman Empire
in the 2nd Century A.D.

ARMENIA
ASSYRIA
MESOPOTAMIA
CAPPADOCIA
SYRIA
ARABIA
GALATIA
CILICIA
JUDAEA
CYPRUS
BITHYNIA & PONTUS
LYCIA & PAMPHYLIA
ASIA
THRACIA
MOESIA INFERIOR
MOESIA SUP.
MACEDONIA
ACHAEA
CRETA
AEGYPTUS
CYRENAICA
DACIA
DALMATIA
PANNONIA
NORICUM
RAETIA
ITALIA
ROME
SICILIA
AFRICA
GERMANIA INFERIOR
AGRI DECUMATES
GERM. SUPERIOR
BELGICA
GALLIA
NARBONENSIS
CORSICA
SARDINIA
NUMIDIA
BRITANNIA
LUGDUNENSIS
AQUITANIA
TARRACONENSIS
HISPANIA
LUSITANIA
BAETICA
MAURETANIA CAESARIENSIS
MAUR. TINGITANA

500 Km
300 M
250
200
100
0
0

4

1. Eternal Rome

Every age has had its own approach to ancient Rome. The city itself was sacked by Goths and Vandals in the fifth century AD, but even then there could still be seen in Rome two colossal statues, 22 equestrian statues, 80 gilded and 74 ivory statues of deities, 36 triumphal arches and 1,785 bronze statues of various kinds. By the fifteenth century, however, only a very few arches and half a dozen bronze statues remained; anything else of intrinsic value had been taken as booty. So desolate was the city that in the twelfth century, Hildebert of Tours could write verses in which the city's ancient grandeur was recalled:

> Rome, thy grand ruins, still beyond compare,
> Thy former greatness mournfully declare,
> Though time thy stately palaces around
> Hath strewed, and cast thy temples to the ground.

Ancient Roman buildings might be converted into churches, and marble fragments from earlier buildings used to adorn them. The re-used green and purple porphyry fragments from the floor of the medieval church of S. Maria in Trastevere (Fig. 1) are a case in point. It was only in the sixteenth century that Rome arose in anything approaching her former splendour.

Fig 1. Green and purple porphyry were among the most costly building materials in ancient Rome. Fragments were re-used in the thirteenth century in the floor of the church of S. Maria in Trastevere (1872.375, H.: 0.110m).

5

The Renaissance: The Renaissance saw a renewal of interest in the ancient world, and it was largely a Roman world that was reborn. Architects, sculptors and painters used Roman models, and they and their patrons observed and collected Roman artefacts. An interesting example is provided by an object known as the Felix Gem (Fig. 49), cut on carnelian, and which was considered to be the most valuable of all the carved gems in the collection of Pope Paul II (1464-71), where it was appraised at 1,000 gold ducats. It next belonged to Cardinal Francesco Gonzaga, who is known to have shown his collection of gems to Andrea Mantegna, the Gonzaga artist in residence, in 1472. Motifs from the Felix Gem occur frequently in Mantegna's work thereafter, and we may assume the artist to have taken impressions from it. (The original purpose of such gems was to serve as seals on documents).

The Felix Gem was made for Calpurnius Severus, a member of the court of the emperor Tiberius (AD 14-37) by the gem cutter Felix. It bears a scene of the seizure of the Palladium — an image of the goddess Pallas Athena (or Minerva) — from the citadel at Troy. Ulysses remonstrates with his companion Diomede- for having murdered Athena's priestess. The reference is to Rome's earliest legendary history: without possession of the Palladium, the Greeks could never take Troy; and without Trojan emigrés (such as Aeneas) there would have been no Rome.

The Arundel Marbles: Later still the Felix Gem was in the collection of Thomas Howard, Earl of Arundel (1585-1646), a person who played a leading role in both art and politics in 17th century England. When he was in Rome in 1613, he was privileged to be allowed to excavate in the Forum and to take the statues he found (said by his enemies to have been planted) home with him to England. He also commissioned four colossal statues in the antique manner from the sculptor Egidio Moretti, who was working for Carlo Maderna on the façade of St. Peter's at the time: two were supposedly of Roman generals, dressed in armour, and two of senators, dressed in what were thought of at the time as togas (Fig. 2). During the next few decades, Arundel assembled a large collection of Greek and Roman sculpture with which he adorned Arundel House, on the Strand in London. Roman sculpture was thought to be imbued with *gravitas* — a concern with order and propriety, with honour and nobility — and its possession was considered to bestow these virtues on the owner. In addition, the houses of princes and cardinals which he had seen on the Continent were frequently decorated with classical, or classicizing, sculpture. Arundel's collection indeed made an impression on contemporaries. King Charles I visited his collection, and the Duke of Buckingham was a rival in collecting ancient sculpture from the eastern Mediterranean. When Sir Francis Bacon visited Arundel House in 1626, "coming into the Earl of Arundel's Garden, where there were a great number of Ancient Statues of naked Men and Women, made a stand, and as astonish'd cryed out: *The Resurrection*".

Fig 3. A tombstone which was probably part of the Arundel collection when it was in London. Originally from Smyrna, it shows Martialis the gladiator as a *retiarius* (he fought with a net and a trident) (Museum of London Loan, H.: 0.515m).

Fig 2. Lord Arundel excavated statues at Rome which he brought back to England with him. He also employed a local craftsman named Egidio Moretti to make four more colossal statues. They included this "senator" dressed in what was thought of in the seventeenth century as a toga (Michaelis 46, H.: 2.08m).

Fig 4. The Arundel Marbles were presented to Oxford University in 1755. The *University Almanack* for 1757 recorded their arrival with a splendid allegorical scene: 'The University... is introduced from her Gothic retirement by Minerva to the Knowledge of... Antiquity, Sculpture, and Architecture'.

The bulk of the Greco-Roman sculpture in the Ashmolean comes from the Arundel collection, but most of the statues spent the years between 1680 and 1755 in Northamptonshire where they adorned the house and gardens at Easton Neston, the seat of the Pomfrets. When Henrietta Louisa, Dowager Countess of Pomfret, became an enthusiast for the Gothic Revival movement (see the memorial to her in the North Porch of the University Church, Oxford), she gave the classical sculpture to Oxford University. The *University Almanack* for 1757 records the arrival of the statues and reliefs in Oxford with a splendid allegorical scene (Fig. 4). One piece of sculpture that did not come by this route is the marble tombstone of Martialis (Fig. 3), a gladiator of the kind known as a *retiarius* (he fought with a net and a trident). Originally from Smyrna in Asia Minor, the tombstone was almost certainly part of the Arundel collection when it was in London, but was subsequently found in the ruins of a house in Islington in 1774, was lost again, and was rediscovered in 1879 during excavations in the Tottenham Court Road.

Inigo Jones: Arundel was an important patron of the arts. The architect Inigo Jones (1573-1652) was a prominent member of his circle, and a pioneer in the introduction of Roman architectural forms into the language of architecture in England. He employed the classical orders to splendid effect in the buildings he designed as Surveyor of the King's Works, and there exists in Oxford, in the Library of Worcester College, a copy of Andrea Palladio's *I quattro libri dell' architettura* (1601) annotated by Jones in 1613 when he accompanied Arundel on his visit to Italy. Jones was to use Palladio's plan and elevation of the Temple of Venus and Rome as the basis for the magnificent portico (with columns 45 feet high) which he built for the facade of Old St Paul's in 1634-42 (Fig. 5), and his classicism also lay behind the Palladian movement which took root in England in the eighteenth century.

The Grand Tour: By the eighteenth century, it had become the norm for English noblemen to adorn their houses and gardens with sculpture from Italy, and much of it was Roman. Since complete statues were desirable but rarely found, it was customary for fragments to be made up into whole figures. Similarly, broken vases and candelabra were enhanced by skilled craftsmen who catered to the requirements of travellers making the Grand Tour. Foremost among these was Giovanni Battista Piranesi, who published many of his restorations in his *Vasi, Candelabri, Cippi* (1778). This work included illustrations of two candelabra made up of fragments from Hadrian's Villa near Tivoli, presented to the University by Sir Roger Newdigate M.P. in 1777. They stood for many years in the Radcliffe Camera before being moved to the Ashmolean. One of them (Fig. 7) is an elaborate construction whose most prominent feature are three cranes which support a kneeling slave who in turn bears the tray upon which a lamp would have stood.

There was a great demand for souvenirs of all kinds on the part of visitors to Italy during the eighteenth century. Small bronze copies of well known Antique statues were made by Italian craftsmen as speculative ventures for aristocratic patrons and other wealthy travellers. The workshops of Massimiliano Soldani (1658-1750), Francesco Righetti (1738-1819) and Giacomo and Giovanni Zoffoli (*c.* 1731-1785; *c.* 1745-1805) made reduced copies of statues in Florence, Rome and Naples as mementos of the Grand Tour. The *Callipygian Venus* (Fig. 6) from Righetti's workshop was a great favourite among the youthful devotees of classicism who made the Grand Tour. It is a version of a statue now in Naples, but in Rome until 1792.

Pompeii and Herculaneum: The eighteenth-century public followed with keen interest the rediscovery of Pompeii and Herculaneum (destroyed during an eruption of Vesuvius in AD 79), and such interest was not simply archaeological. The destruction of Lisbon in an earthquake in 1755 had shocked civilised Europe,

Fig 5. The architect Inigo Jones was a member of Arundel's circle, and visited Italy with him. Jones used Andrea Palladio's plan and elevation of the Temple of Venus and Rome as the basis for the portico of Old St Paul's (from W. Kent, *Designs of Inigo Jones* [1727]).

and the somewhat macabre publications of the excavations at Pompeii and Herculaneum helped people imagine what horrors Lisbon must have experienced. In *Candide*, Voltaire used Lisbon to suggest that the old order might after all change, as indeed it did with the French Revolution. The resurrected cities were extremely popular with tourists through the nineteenth century, and remain so down to the present day. Many finds are in the Naples and Pompeii museums, but many more found their way into the hands of dealers and collectors. A few bronze vessels (e.g. Fig. 8) and fresco fragments are in the Ashmolean.

Fig 7. An engraving by G.B. Piranesi of a Roman candelabrum from Hadrian's Villa at Tivoli which he restored in his workshop at Rome (from *Vasi, Candelabri, Cippi* [1778]). The original is in Oxford.

Fig 6. The *Callipygian Venus* by Francesco Righetti is a version of a statue now in Naples, but in Rome until 1792, and is typical of the bronze statuettes that were made as souvenirs for wealthy travellers on the Grand Tour (Penny 79, H. 0.345m).

Fig 8. A bronze jug which was probably found at Pompeii, the Roman city destroyed in the eruption of Vesuvius in AD 79, and whose rediscovery was followed with great interest by the 18th century public (1932.191, L.: 0.150m).

Pilgrimage: Rome was and is a major centre of Christian pilgrimage, but it is uncertain whether a series of lamps representing St. Peter's encounter with Christ on the outskirts of Rome were deliberate forgeries or simply sold as "aids to faith". They may well have been made in order to take advantage of the success of Henryk Sienkiewicz's *Quo Vadis*, first published in 1896, for they are inscribed in Latin: DOMINE QUO VADIS ("Lord, whither goest Thou?") and VENIO ROMAM ITERUM CRUCIFIGI ("I am coming to Rome to be crucified again").

Forgeries: Rather more sinister are the forgeries of moulds for Arretine pottery (relief-decorated ceramics made at Arezzo in north central Italy in the first centuries BC and AD) made around 1900. The erotic subject-matter of many of these moulds (Fig. 9) appealed to collectors of *curiosa*, but it was only in the late 1980s that scientific tests showed that the bulk of such pieces in museums throughout Europe and North America were modern forgeries. In the meantime, they had provided the foundation for the study of Arretine pottery, research on which has now to be reassessed.

Fig 9. A mould for Arretine pottery made *c.* 1900, but only shown to be a modern forgery in the 1980s. The subject-matter of many of these moulds appealed to collectors of a certain cast of mind (1966.252, D.: 0.22m).

2. The Countryside

The poems of Virgil and Horace are full of praises of the Italian countryside during the early Empire. Ausonius describes the delights of the Moselle in later times. A country villa provided both a source of income for the landowner, and a retreat from the heat of the city in the summer.

Pliny's Villa: Pliny the Younger has left a long description of his own estate at Laurentum near Rome which gives us an idea of how pleasant the country residence of a wealthy Roman might have been. A model based on Pliny's description (Fig. 21), made by the late Clifford Pember ARIBA in the 1940s, is especially popular with younger visitors to the Ashmolean. It is interesting to note that the actual villa was discovered in the 1980s in excavations at Grotte di Piastra, 17 miles south of Rome, and that the Ashmolean's model differs only in minor respects. There were colonnades, courtyards, a dining room, and a room "whose windows admit sun all day long; set in the wall of this room is a cupboard like a bookcase containing books that should be reread, not merely read". Next to this was a bedroom "connected to a passageway with a hollow floor and walls fitted with pipes from which it receives hot air". A bath suite, a tower with a view along the coast, more bedrooms, shaded but airy galleries, servants' quarters, and beautiful gardens complete the picture.

Problems of survival: Most material of intrinsic value will long since have been removed, sold off, or looted from a Roman residential site, and marble will have gone into the lime kiln or been used to adorn a later building. It is thus scarcely surprising that the village church near the Villa of Tiberius on Capri boasts a splendid marble floor. Some extremely luxurious villas even had silver water pipes, but usually all we are left with is largely unrecyclable material such as potsherds, broken bricks and tiles, and fragments of plaster — scarcely an adequate cross-section of what used to be there. In Britain, even the walls of Roman buildings have disappeared, but then few medieval monastic sites were more than a few miles from a Roman structure: it is clear both where the building stone came from and why most Romano-British sites are denuded of masonry.

We can, nevertheless, use the surviving remains to assist us to envisage country life in the Roman world: for the rich, a world of elegant surroundings, and of ease. Thus painted plaster cornices can help us envision carved and coloured marble architectural decoration, and terracotta ("baked clay") reliefs something of the profusion of decorative friezes on both the inside and outside of country villas, town houses, baths, temples and tombs. The materials used for wall decoration varied according to the status of the owner: inlaid exotic marble and mosaics set the tone, but most walls (and certainly most extant walls) were decorated in fresco (painting done on plaster) which was much cheaper. Fashions in wall decoration changed too: sometimes there was a taste for wholly

Fig 10. A bronze fitting in the form of a donkey's head which once decorated the curved part (*fulcrum*) of a Roman couch. Wild donkeys, like the lions and panthers which also appear on furniture, were hunted for sport in the ancient Near East (1976.572, H.: 0.15m).

Fig 11. A bronze leg from a Roman chair. Its turned appearance recalls furniture made from ivory and exotic woods (1932.442, H.: 0.31m).

architectural designs, at others for an illusionistic treatment of nature, with gardens and fantastic vistas to be seen in the distance. Sometimes, too, "pictures" might be set within a large expanse of plain wall. The more public rooms of a Roman house might be more elaborately decorated than the private and domestic areas.

Furniture: The furniture of a Roman house was rather different from what we are used to today. A dining room would be equipped with a set of couches on which guests would recline. Tables would be set in front, and heating in winter supplied from a brazier. Bedrooms were small, and would have a bed, chests for clothes and blankets, and perhaps a table and chair or stool. But for all its apparent simplicity, Roman furniture could be highly decorated and made from luxurious materials. We hear about gold, ivory, and silver furniture in Roman literature, but only bronze fittings have survived in any quantity. These would, however, originally have been highly polished, if not actually gilded, so as to resemble gold. The curved parts of couches (*fulcra*) were often adorned with modelled heads of lions, panthers or donkeys (Fig. 10). Legs might be turned (or if in bronze [Fig. 11] appear to be turned), recalling the forms of furniture made from ivory and exotic woods.

Tableware ideally consisted of gold vessels, but few people could afford them, and scarcely any examples have survived from antiquity: only three, all of which came out of the sea off Cnidus in the 1890s. Silverware has survived in greater quantity, although again many pieces will have gone into the melting pot. Weight and purity were the prime considerations; artistry on the part of the silversmith might

14

Fig 12. An Arretine drinking bowl with reliefs of lovers made at Arezzo, Central Italy in the later first century BC or the early first century AD. Fine red-glaze pottery was made throughout the Roman Empire as a reflection of gold tableware (1966.250, H.: 0.145m)

add to the value of a vessel, but only for as long as the decoration was fashionable. If it were not, plate would be melted down and remade. Hard-stone vessels too were highly prized in the Roman world: they might be made from rock crystal, sardonyx, porphyry, or simply marble.

Imitation: Most frequently, we are left with cheaper imitations of expensive materials. Pewter vessels (pp. 21-2) attest to the prevalence of silverware. Skilful potters made fine red-glaze pottery throughout the Roman Empire (e.g. Arretine [Fig. 12], South and Central Gaulish, North African red slip-ware) as a reflection of the gold vessels on the tables of the rich. Grey and black fine pottery was made in evocation of silver vessels (Fig. 13), and even relatively inexpensive bronze was imitated by potters. There is thus a category of glazed pottery, yellow on the

15

inside and green on the outside, which is widely thought to have been made to resemble bronze vessels which were cleaned within and left dirty without (Fig. 14).

Agriculture: Pliny's villa was primarily for residential use. Most villas, however, were centres of agricultural activity worked by slaves in a manner similar to plantations in the American south before the Civil War. Such villas would be largely self-sufficient enterprises, making their own tiles and bricks, their own iron tools, and their own cloth. The commodities they produced might change in response to the demands of the market. Thus, excavations have shown that the Roman villa at Settefinestre near Cosa in Northern Italy produced grain, oil, and wine during the later first century BC and the first century AD, but ceased to produce wine and oil in the second century, for these could then be imported more cheaply from the provinces. Instead, slaves became a commodity in their own right, and were bred and sold.

Shakenoak, Oxfordshire: None of the material from Settefinestre is in Oxford, but the Ashmolean is fortunate in having many of the finds from a Roman villa site at Shakenoak, near North Leigh, Oxfordshire. The villa was one of several in the area, and is interesting for a number of reasons. It was continuously occupied from the last quarter of the first century AD until the middle of the eighth century, and thus spans both the Roman and Anglo-Saxon periods in Britain. Like Settefinestre, its functions changed over the centuries. The development of the villa up to the beginning of the third century seems to indicate a steadily rising prosperity reflected in an expanding agricultural establishment (the so-called "Building A") and a dwelling-house ("Building B") that grew in size and comfort throughout this period. However in the later Roman period alterations to "Building A" made it a well-appointed dwelling house complete with baths (Fig. 15) and window glass (Fig. 17), while "Building B" became dilapidated and was later partly demolished.

A notable feature of Shakenoak is the presence, from the middle of the second century AD, of a series of fishponds designed for the breeding of fresh-water fish, presumably trout. No other Romano-British villa has produced this kind of arrangement, but it does seem to have been in principle the fore-runner of the modern trout farm. The largest pond ("Fishpond II") measured about 65.5 x 27 metres. The dampness of the earth with which it subsequently silted up contributed to the preservation over the centuries of a good deal of ancient worked timber: 200 planks of oak — some as long as 3 metres — more than 1,000 laths, and several off-cuts of beams. Waste in such large quantities must reflect the low value placed on cut timber in this part of the Roman world at the time. In the silt of Fishpond II was a hinged flap or sluice (Fig. 16) which has been interpreted as part of a device to allow water to flow through a pipe in one direction, while preventing fish from travelling in the other. Other finds included painted plaster, window glass, leatherwork, pottery,

Fig 13. A Roman silver bowl and grey pottery wares made as a cheap version of silver (R. 286, H.: 0.046m; 1990.93, D.: 0.089m; R. 287, H.: 0.036m).

Fig 14. Roman potters even imitated relatively inexpensive bronze. These glazed bowls are yellow on the inside, and green on the outside, achieving the effect of clean and corroded bronze to be seen on the jug in the centre (1990.145, H.: 0.086m; 1879.372, H.: 0.183m; 1970.361, H.: 0.057m).

Fig 15. Building A at Shakenoak, a Roman villa complex near North Leigh in Oxfordshire. This reconstruction shows the building as a well-appointed dwelling house complete with baths: the way it appeared in the mid-fourth century AD (after Brodribb, Hands and Walker).

Fig 16. An oakwood hinged flap or sluice from one of the fishponds at Shakenoak: a device to allow water to flow through a pipe in one direction, while preventing fish from travelling in the other (1974.316, H.: 0.12m).

Fig 17. Fragments of window glass from the Roman villa at Shakenoak (1972.15.20, greatest dimension 0.190m).

18

bronze fragments and many iron tools. The latter were especially interesting as iron is rarely well preserved.

Ironwork: Advances in conservation techniques during the past few decades has meant that the Ashmolean has a good deal of Roman ironwork, not simply from Shakenoak, but from other local centres as well. Iron was a material of great importance in the Roman period, being used for weapons, agricultural implements, tools, chains, and strengthening bands on doors, furniture, vehicles, buckets and barrels. Iron ore was available from several centres in Britain. The role of the blacksmith was probably much the same in antiquity as at any period down to the early part of this century, and workers in many other occupations depended on his skill and industry for the tools of their own trades.

One of the most spectacular pieces of Roman ironwork to have survived is a chain from Appleford (Fig. 18), the knot-work and double-links of which find parallels elsewhere in Roman Britain: at Cirencester, Winchester, Silchester and among a hoard of late Roman ironwork from Great Chesterford, in Essex (now in the Cambridge University Museum of Archaeology and Ethnology). Double-links of the same type were used for making fine gold chains for jewellery in all parts of the Empire, but for ironwork, apparently only in Britain. Fragments of a chain of this sort survived to form a part of the 12-foot cauldron chain in the seventh century AD Sutton Hoo barrow. Other iron objects from Appleford include a padlock, a steelyard, a shovel handle, and two fragments of a long scythe blade. Another group of iron objects was found at Dorchester-on-Thames overlying the

Fig 18. A Roman iron chain found in a gravel pit at Appleford. The links are made out of a single ring of metal; they do not interlink with each other as on an ordinary chain (Amey Construction Loan, L.: 1.5m).

Fig 19. A jug, bowl and plates; some of the twenty-four Roman pewter vessels found together with ironwork at Appleford in 1968. They had probably been hidden in a well which collapsed and silted up when the site was abandoned in antiquity (Amey Construction Loan, D. of largest plate: 0.45m).

Fig 20. A stone pewter mould from St Just in Cornwall, a county rich in tin, the principal ingredient of the pewter alloy (1836.147-8, H.: 0.082m).

Fig 21. A model by the late Clifford Pember ARIBA based on Pliny the Younger's description of his suburban seaside villa at Laurentum near Rome (1962.37, 0.90 x 0.90m).

last street surface, in the silt washed from the back of the southern rampart of the Roman settlement. They include fragments of ploughshares and date from the late fourth century onwards, and they illustrate the kind of equipment current in fourth-century British farming communities.

Pewter: The Appleford ironwork was found together with a large hoard of pewter vessels, and the whole assemblage is exhibited at the Ashmolean thanks to the continued generosity of Amey Construction, in one of whose gravel pits it was found in 1968. In times of danger sets of pewter vessels might be hidden from a predator. In times of exceptional danger the owner might fail to return to collect his property, and it would be left to be found by chance later on. This is what almost certainly occurred with the twenty-four pewter vessels — plates, bowls and a jug (Fig. 19) — from Appleford. They had probably been hidden in a well which had collapsed and silted up when the site was abandoned. The shapes and decorative motifs recall those on silverware of the fourth century AD (such as the Mildenhall Treasure in the British Museum). The Appleford and other pewter hoards in Britain seem to have been deposited during a very disturbed period at the end of the fourth century.

The largest plate in the Appleford pewter hoard has a Latin inscription scratched on the underside: PACATA EMITA PARTA SUA LOVERNIANUS DONAVIT. The word PACATA differs from the rest of the inscription; it is written in the same way as that on one of the smaller plates. It is presumably a woman's name — perhaps a former owner of the plates. If the remainder of the inscription, EMITA is miswritten for EMPTA; the translation reads: "Lovernianus gave his purchases as a gift". Lovernianus is a latinized form of a Celtic name, and means "Son of a fox". The finds from Woodeaton (pp.44-5) attest to the survival of Celtic traditions in Roman Britain.

Thanks to this material and to a much earlier benefactor, the Rev. William Borlase (1695-1772), the Cornish antiquary, the Ashmolean has a remarkable display of Roman pewter. Pewter vessels were often cast in stone moulds such as the example from St Just (Fig. 20) in Cornwall, a county rich in tin, the principal ingredient (with lead, or less frequently, copper) of the pewter alloy. Also from Cornwall came a jug and bowl, found in a well at St Erth. A pewter dish, found on the University Farm at Wytham reflects prevailing fashions in Britain in the fourth century AD. In antiquity pewter served as "poor man's silver". The houses of the rich might have had dressers stacked with gold or silver vessels: more modest establishments will have made do with bronze or pewter, or even pottery. There is the story of the emperor Vitellius, when still a general, seizing the silver plate of a temple in North Africa, and replacing it with pewter vessels.

Fig 22. A bronze horse muzzle adorned with delicately engraved serpents and added bronze snakes (1971.833, L.: 0.240m).

Fig 23. The Wint Hill bowl is made of glass, a cheap substitute for rock-crystal. It is engraved with a hunting scene. A hare is driven into a net by a horseman and two hounds (1957.168, D.: 0.193m).

Horsemanship: The horse was a high-status riding animal (oxen and mules were used for pulling heavy carts and wagons), and great pains were taken by owners to ensure that their mounts were elegantly equipped. Padded saddles rested on colourful saddle-cloths and the horses' leather trappings might be enhanced with gold, silver or bronze roundels and pendants. Only base metal (bronze or iron) harness fittings tend to have survived. Sometimes, however, they can be very ornate. A bronze muzzle in the Ashmolean is adorned with added bronze snakes and bears delicately engraved serpents (Fig. 22). A smaller muzzle is rather simpler: it carries rings which were used to attach it to the headstall. An iron prick spur is of a type known from Hod Hill, Dorset, a site occupied for only the first 20 years of the Roman occupation of Britain which began in AD 43.

Hunting: In Roman antiquity — especially in the later Empire (in the third and fourth centuries) — hunting was a major country activity, and scenes of the chase figure large, especially in the art of the late Roman period. Mosaics and drinking vessels of the third and fourth centuries are frequently decorated with hunting scenes. The Wint Hill glass bowl is engraved with a hare hunt (Fig. 23). A horseman and two hounds drive a hare into a net. The inscriptions are partly in Latin and partly in Greek (the languages of the western and eastern parts of the Roman empire respectively): "Long life to you and yours" and "Drink and good health to you".

23

3. The City

About the year 150 AD, the orator Aelius Aristides, himself a native of Mysia in Asia Minor, idealized the Roman empire in fulsome terms: "A single rivalry obsesses every city — to appear as beautiful and attractive as possible. Every place is full of gymnasia, fountains and gateways, temples, shops, and schools... Cities shine in radiance and beauty". Of his own part of the world, he tells the emperor: "Now under you all the Greek cities emerge. All the monuments, works of art and adornments in them mean glory for you. Seashore and interior are filled with cities... Ionia, the great prize, is rid of garrisons and satraps, and stands out as a model of elegance to the world. She now outstrips her old self by as much as she was formerly reputed to be ahead of other peoples in taste and refinement."

A century or so earlier, the Greek geographer Strabo wrote in similar vein: "If the Greeks had the repute of being most felicitous in the founding of cities, in that they aimed at beauty, strength of position, harbours, and productive soil, the Romans had best foresight in those matters which the Greeks took but little account of, such as the construction of roads and aqueducts, and of sewers that could wash out the filth of the city into the Tiber... The sewers, vaulted with close-fitting stones, have in some places left room enough for wagons loaded with hay to pass through them. And water is brought into the city through the aqueducts in such quantities that veritable rivers flow through the city and the sewers; and almost every house has cisterns and service pipes and copious fountains...."

Water supply: Claudius (emperor AD 41-54) undertook but a few major public works compared with the activities of some of his predecessors (Augustus [emperor 31 BC - AD 14] claimed to have found Rome a city of brick and left it a city of marble). But foremost among Claudius' achievements was the construction of a harbour at Ostia and the provision of a new water supply for the city of Rome: "He brought to the city on stone arches the cool and abundant springs of the Claudian aqueduct ... and at the same time the channel of the New Anio, distributing them into many beautifully ornamented fountains." Near the Aqua Claudia, outside the Porta Maggiore to the south of the city, was found a large fragment of lead piping (Fig. 24) some 10 cms in diameter. It is inscribed in Latin as follows: "The Emperor Caesar Augustus Vespasian's pipeline, laid by the procurator Callistus, a freedman of the Augustus".

The care and administration of the water supply of Rome was under the supervision of the *curator aquarum*. His duties included the maintenance of the aqueducts, reservoirs and pipelines, the control of the supply, and the prevention of illegal tapping. To guard against the latter all new pipes were

Fig 24. A fragment of lead water pipe found near the Aqua Claudia, outside the Porta Maggiore to the south of Rome. It bears the Latin inscription: "The Emperor Caesar Augustus Vespasian's pipeline, laid by the procurator Callistus, a freedman of the Augustus" (1924.8, L.: 0.037m).

stamped along their length. The pipe in Oxford is dated to Vespasian's principate, AD 69-79. Callistus is described as a procurator, a deputy working for the *curator aquarum;* such posts were frequently held by freed slaves during the first century. We know from other sources that Callistus was still working under Domitian (AD 79-96). Other examples of the same stamp come from a pipeline in the VIIth region of ancient Rome. The stamps were placed at each end of the lengths of pipe, and each length was numbered, the numbers being stamped in large letters after the inscription.

Frontinus who was *curator aquarum* at the end of the first century, wrote a full account of the water supply and of the duties of his office. He includes a list of the standard sizes of pipe. The Oxford fragment corresponds to a *"vicenaria"*, which could deliver sixteen *"quinariae"* — one *"quinaria"* being the standard delivery to a private dwelling.

Grain supply: The Roman poet Lucan wrote that "the grain supply provides the mainsprings of hatred and popularity. Hunger alone sets cities free, and reverence is purchased when rulers feed the lazy mob: a hungry populace knows no fear". Fear of food riots, and the actual experience of a severe famine, encouraged Claudius to build a new harbour at Ostia, at the mouth of the Tiber so that grain could be imported all the year round. "He built curving breakwaters on the right and the left", says Suetonius, "while before the entrance he placed a jetty in deep water. To give this jetty a firmer foundation he first sank the ship in which the great obelisk had been brought from Egypt [the obelisk which now stands in the centre of St Peter's Square in Rome], and then securing it by piles built upon it a very lofty tower after the model of the Pharos at Alexandria, to be lighted at night and guide the course of the ships".

Fig 25. A bronze sestertius issued by Nero in AD 64 shows something of the arrangements at Portus, the new harbour at Ostia built by his predecessor Claudius to enable grain to be imported all the year round (Heberden Coin Room, D.: 0.033m).

Claudius' achievement was commemorated on coins issued by his successor, Nero. A bronze sestertius issued in AD 64 shows a bird's eye view (Fig. 25) of the arrangements at Portus (as the new harbour was called). Neptune, personifying the sea, reclines in the foreground, while behind him are ships and colonnaded harbour buildings. Another coin commemorating the same event shows figures of Annona, a personification of the grain supply, and Ceres, the corn goddess, with the prow of a merchantman between them.

26

Fig 26. A brick bearing the stamp of Ianuarius, the manager of a brickworks belonging to Domitia Lucilla, a lady who took over the control of the potworks of the gens Domitia when her adopted father died in AD 108 (1872.1513, H. of stamp: 0.033m).

Building programmes: Building in Roman cities was frequently conducted on a grandiose scale, whether by the municipality or as the result of private or imperial patronage. The object was to create public works projects in order to provide employment for the populace, as well as to provide baths, temples, theatres, amphitheatres, circuses, public squares (*fora*) and indoor meeting places (*basilicae*) for the community at large. One of the advantages of life in a city in the Roman empire was the availability of baths (*thermae*). At Rome itself, emperors built increasingly spacious and grand public baths. The Baths of Titus were built rather hurriedly to accompany the opening of the nearby Colosseum in AD 80. They were constructed over the site of what had been the Golden House of Nero, in the substructures of which were found in the seventeenth century some fresco panels with mythological scenes. One of these is now in Oxford, having been in the collection of Dr Richard Mead (1673-1754) in London. It shows (Fig. 28) the offering of Adonis to Venus after his birth from a tree. Venus was the legendary ancestor of the *gens Julia* (the family of Julius Caesar) with which the Claudii, Nero's family had intermarried.

Brickworks: Nero's Golden House at Rome was built after the great fire of AD 64, an event in which the emperor was implicated, although there is no evidence that he was responsible, nor that he "fiddled while Rome burned". Such was the destruction wrought during the fire, however, that there was an enormous demand for bricks for new buildings. Many well known families, whose estates in the Tiber valley contained extensive clay beds, were engaged in the profitable business of brickmaking. Many bricks bear stamps with the names of the owners and managers of brickworks. One in Oxford has the stamp of Ianuarius who worked for Domitia Lucilla, a lady who took over the control of the potteries of the gens Domitia when her adopted father died in AD 108 (Fig. 26). Between AD 110 and 160 brickstamps were often dated by the addition of the consuls' names. Another stamp in Oxford reads: "From the Quintanensian estates of Annius Verus, made by Pomponius Vitalis during the consulships of Apronianus and Paetinus" — i.e. in AD 123.

Houses: Most houses in Rome were notoriously unsafe; shoddily built and liable to be destroyed in one of the frequent fires. The poet Juvenal contrasted the houses at "cool Praeneste, or at Volsinii among the wooded hills, or at simple Gabii, or on the heights of sloping Tivoli" with those at Rome: "We inhabit a city supported to a great extent by slender props; for in this way the building manager saves the houses from falling. And when he has plastered over the gaping hole of an old crack, he bids us sleep securely, with ruin overhanging us... Already your third storey is smoking; you yourself know nothing about it; for if the alarm begins from the bottom of the stairs, the last man to know there is a fire will be the one who is protected from the rain only by the roof tiles." Little has survived from such structures.

Vaulting techniques: More substantial buildings incorporated arches and vaults, and Roman architects developed some ingenious techniques to reduce the weight (and expense) of roofs. Sometimes they used tufa (a light volcanic stone) or empty amphoras set within concrete. In the second century AD, a system of interlocking pottery tubes was developed which was used extensively in North Africa. These tubes, interlocking and cemented together, required little or nothing in the way of timber supports for their erection, and once set, provided a framework on which the remainder of the vault could be constructed. The same technique was employed at Ravenna for the construc-

Fig 27. Bronze letters belonging to a dedicatory inscription to the emperor Hadrian on the Roman city gate at Antalya (the ancient Attaleia) in southwestern Asia Minor (1884.531, H.: 0.140m).

Fig 28. A fragment of a fresco from the Golden House of Nero at Rome. It shows the offering of Adonis to Venus after his birth from a tree. Venus was the legendary ancestor of the *gens Julia* with which the Claudii, the family of Nero had intermarried (1930.751, H.: 0.90m).

tion of complete domes: a double spiral of tubes being built up into a dome, like a straw bee-hive. Examples of such tubes from Beauvais in France, and from Carthage and Bulla Regia in Tunisia are to be seen in the Ashmolean.

City gates: Many Roman cities had ceremonial gateways — it was only towards the end of the Roman empire with the threat of invasion from beyond the frontiers that cities needed to be fortified at all. The city gate at Antalya (the ancient Attaleia) in southwestern Asia Minor (modern Turkey) was built in order to commemorate the visit of the emperor Hadrian in AD 130. It was a triple arched gateway and carried two dedications, in Greek, to Hadrian. One of these was in letters of bronze (Fig. 27) on the architrave and was probably the dedication of the gate itself. Some of these letters were given to the Ashmolean in 1884.

Taxation: There were elaborate systems of direct municipal and provincial taxation in the Roman empire, as well as indirect taxes such as customs duties and transit tolls. Occasionally emperors resorted to a wholesale cancellation of tax arrears as a means of enhancing their popularity. Hadrian, for example, proudly claimed on coins "nine hundred million sesterces in old arrears cancelled". Much of our detailed information concerning personal taxation comes from Roman Egypt. Thousands of tax receipts survive written in Greek on scraps of broken pottery (*ostraca*). These are typical: (1) "Siaitus, son of Maiyris. You have paid 10 dr. for poll tax. Year 10 of Caesar". (2) "Harpaesis, son of Phenophis, has paid the remaining 9 drachmas for poll tax of year 2 of Trajan the lord. Written by me, Hermogenes, tax collector" (Fig. 29). (3) "Didymion, collector, represented by Palachemis. Petorzmethis, son of Petorzmethis and Senpachnubis, grandson of Petorzmethis, has paid for poll tax of the fifth year of Hadrian Caesar the lord seventeen drachmae 1/2 obol, and for the prison guards 1/2 obol, = 17 dr. 1 ob. Hathyr 3."

Fig 29. A tax receipt from Roman Egypt. Written in Greek on a potsherd (*ostracon*), it reads: "Harpaesis, son of Phenophis, has paid the remaining 9 drachmas for poll tax of year 2 of Trajan the lord. Written by me, Hermogenes, tax collector"
(Ashm. G.O. 229, greatest dimension: 0.10m).

4. The People

Roman society was firmly hierarchical, with greatest honour accorded to free citizen families who had served the state in battle, or who possessed great wealth. The *honestiores* were those who possessed "property, power and prestige"; the *humiliores* included slaves, freedmen, and free born citizens who did not possess sufficient influence to protect their property-rights in law. Women shared the status of their fathers and husbands, but could neither vote nor hold political office. Marriages were usually arranged by the parents of the couple, and divorce was common, although at times officially discouraged. Children were regarded as small adults, and their education was concerned in the main with preparing them for public life, for marriage, or for labour. Slaves, who were in effect the cheap power supply of antiquity, suffered from the additional burden of being considered to be property themselves. They worked on farms, in factories, as oarsmen on ships, and as miners and quarrymen. Skilled slaves might work in craftsmen's workshops, as scribes and copyists or as domestic workers. Freed slaves (*liberti* or "freedmen") had a special status, and some of them became extremely wealthy.

Men: Roman family life was, in principle, robust. A father had the right of life and death over his offspring, and could even sell them into slavery. But the poets occasionally give us glimpses of the tender side of Roman family life. Lucretius, writing about a man close to death, says: "No more shall your glad home welcome you, nor your good wife and sweet children rush to snatch the first kisses and to touch your heart with a silent thrill of joy". Usually, however, we hear only of more serious matters: legal business, wills, dowries. The law, moreover, was a good way for an ambitious young (male) Roman to get on in the world. Cicero, for example, made his name in the lawcourts before rising to the consulate (consuls — two per year — being the highest elected officials in the Roman state).

The characteristic garment of a Roman citizen was the toga, a long mantle worn over a tunic (e.g. Fig. 31). In that it consisted of a large segmental piece of material about 5.5 metres long and 2 metres deep at its widest point, it must have been difficult to put on without assistance. Youths under 16 and magistrates had a scarlet or purple stripe along the straight edge, candidates for office wore pure white, and mourners black or a dark colour. The head would be covered with a fold of the toga when a sacrifice to the gods was performed. Ordinary folk simply wore a tunic.

Clothing was expensive, and only the rich had an extensive wardrobe. Trousers were regarded as barbaric, and as late as AD 397 it was illegal to wear them in the city of Rome. In cold weather, a cloak might be worn over the toga.

Fig 30. A Roman terracotta statuette of the third century AD of a woman (perhaps Venus) holding a comb in one hand and a mirror in the other. She wears earrings, a necklace and bracelets, as well as a long cloak over a tunic (1973.962, H.: 0.59m).

Women: Rich women spent fortunes on dresses, the form of which remained the same for centuries, but — as with Indian saris — scope for fashion lay in the variety of colour and decoration available to those who could afford costly fabrics. Fine textiles have rarely survived from antiquity (more typical is a piece of rough tweed found in a well in a Roman signal station in Yorkshire, and now shared between the Ashmolean and several other museums). The archaeological record relating to women consists in the main of grave goods: combs, hair pins, mirrors, and jewellery. Painting and sculpture can help to fill out the picture. A third century AD terracotta statuette shows a woman (perhaps Venus) holding a comb in one hand and a mirror in the other (Fig. 30). She wears earrings, a necklace and bracelets, as well as a long cloak over a tunic. Roman mirrors often had elaborate backs: one in Oxford is decorated with Europa and the Bull (Fig. 33), and another with Eros. Mirrors often had covers to protect the reflecting surface from scratches.

Perfumes and cosmetics in Roman antiquity could be expensive and exotic, with ingredients often imported from beyond the bounds of the empire, notably frankincense from Arabia and cassia from India. Men used perfumes as well. Containers might also be made from exotic materials: gold, rock crystal, silver, ivory, amber; cheaper ones from bronze, bone, glass or pottery. The extravagance of some Roman matrons

Fig 32. A marble statue of a man wearing a toga, the characteristic garment of a Roman citizen. The toga was a mantle about 5.5 metres long and 2 metres deep at its widest point, worn over a tunic (Michaelis 45; H.: 2.08m).

Fig 33. Roman mirror-back, decorated with the myth of Europa and the Bull. Europa was a princess of Tyre in what is now Lebanon. Jupiter fell in love with her, changed himself into a bull, and carried her off over the sea (1971.822, D.: 0.137m).

Fig 32. A gold *bulla*, the amulet worn by freeborn Roman children until they reached maturity. This example was found at Herculaneum and was presented by the Neapolitan court to the empress Josephine (Oldfield 1, H.: 0.10m).

was satirized by Lucian: "[A lady] must, these days, use powders, pomades, paints... each chambermaid carries one of the essential objects for the toilette. One holds a silver basin, another a chamber pot, a third a water pot; still others the mirror and as many boxes as one could find in a pharmacy; and all these boxes contain only things she would not want anyone to see. In one are teeth and drugs for the gums; in others, eyelashes and eyebrows and the means of restoring faded beauty". The poet Ovid was more discreet: "while you are at your toilette let us think that you are asleep; it is more fitting that you should be seen when the last touch has been given".

Children: "Only a rich man keeps more than two daughters" was a proverb in antiquity. Unwanted infants were regularly exposed to die, but the practice was condemned by Jews and Christians, and gradually died out. Again, much of the archaeological evidence for children and childhood activities comes from graves. Toys (such as the wooden dove on wheels [Fig. 34], or the model farmyard animals also in the Ashmolean) were placed in the tombs of children. A child's sock (Fig. 35) comes from a similar source. It is not knitted, but made by the technique known as "nalbinding", an ancient method of producing a length of fabric using a needle loaded with a short length of yarn. It closely resembles knitting, but the technique is different.

From infancy the children of a Roman citizen would wear an amulet known as a *bulla* around their neck as a symbol of their free birth. The custom seems to have been inherited by the Romans from the Etruscans. When a boy came of age and cut his childhood locks, a ceremony was held (in the spring) at which he would lay the *bulla* in the household shrine (*lararium*) and assume the dress of manhood (the *toga virilis*). A girl would wear her *bulla* until marriage. Most *bullae* were made from leather or cloth and thus do not survive today. Occasionally, however, *bullae* of more durable materials are found; there are two gold examples in Oxford. One of them (Fig. 32) has an interesting history in its own right. Found at Herculaneum, presumably in a household shrine, it was presented by the Neapolitan court to Napoleon's wife, the empress Josephine.

Freedmen and slaves: In the later Roman empire, the children of freedmen were also permitted to use the *bulla*. A graphic, though exaggerated account of what it was like to be a successful freedman can be found in Petronius' *Satyricon*, where Trimalchio describes his rise to immense wealth: "My good management brought me to my present good fortune... I became master in the house...and got a senator's fortune... I built five ships and loaded them with wine... In one day Neptune swallowed up 30,000,000 sesterces...at this point [my wife] did the loyal thing: she sold all her jewellery, all her dresses, and gave me 100 gold pieces...On one voyage I made 100,000,000 sesterces...everything I touched grew like a honeycomb".

Many skilled slaves seem to have been of Greek origin, captured in Roman

Fig 34. A Roman toy wooden dove on wheels from a child's grave at Hawara in Egypt (1888.763, L.: 0.165m).

Fig 35. A Roman child's sock, preserved in the exceptionally dry climate of Egypt. It is not knitted, but was made by the technique known as nalbinding (1914.622, L.: 0.110m).

Fig 36. A small bronze vase and two inkpots containing the remains of red and black ink, found in the grave of a Roman scribe in Crete (1969.572-574, H. of vase: 0.10m).

campaigns in the eastern Mediterranean. Their arrival on the scene in the closing decades of the Republic attracted much criticism from old-fashioned Romans. Some Roman politicians are known to have expressed anti-Hellenic views in public, but were content to enjoy eastern Mediterranean luxury in private. Just as the intellectual life of Rome was greatly influenced by Greece at that period, so too everyday life — at least for the rich — underwent great changes by the availability of goldsmiths, engravers, musicians, hairdressers, perfumers, cooks, secretaries, or dancing girls. They could be very expensive: the price depending upon the skills they possessed and what a potential owner was prepared to pay. Secretaries in the Roman world were male, and often slaves. Some bronze objects in the Ashmolean, which include a small bronze vase and two inkpots containing the remains of red and black ink, were found in the grave of a scribe in Crete (Fig. 36).

Most slaves were employed in agriculture or mining — both important sectors of the Roman economy. Miners had to open shafts and to seek out seams rich in silver, gold, copper or other ores. A pick, lamp and wedge in Oxford come from a Roman mine at Sizma in Asia Minor. For all their importance in the Roman world, actual representations of slaves are uncommon. A limestone mould from Roman Egypt was for making statuettes of an actor playing the part of a slave. A marble relief in the Ashmolean (Fig. 37) shows pairs of slaves wearing metal collars and being led on ropes by helmeted figures. The precise purpose of the relief, which is said to come from Smyrna, is uncertain, but it gives us an insight into the hardships that might be experienced by unskilled slaves in antiquity.

Fig 37. A Roman marble relief from Smyrna showing pairs of slaves wearing metal collars and led on ropes by helmeted figures. Small wonder there were periodic slave revolts in the Greco-Roman world (Michaelis 137, H.: 0.99m).

5. The Gods

Religion played a highly important part in Roman life, whether public or private. The destiny of the Roman state was thought to be controlled by deities who were worshipped in temples in which priests conducted sacrifices in their honour. The welfare of the family too was thought to be in the hands of household gods who were venerated on a daily basis. In its proliferation of deities, the Roman world will have been much closer to modern India than to the monotheistic Christian, Jewish and Islamic worlds. Roman emperors might be worshipped as gods. Rulers in the Hellenistic East had long laid claim to divine honours. Roman emperors encouraged the continuance of the ruler cult in the eastern empire and fostered its spread in the West, but in ways which were in keeping with Roman religious traditions.

The most important temple at Rome was on the Capitoline Hill. It was built in the Etruscan manner with three divisions, occupied by images of Jupiter, Juno and Minerva — the Roman equivalents of the Greek Zeus, Hera and Athena. Splendid sacrifices and games were celebrated in honour of the Capitoline triad, as they were called. Jupiter's outward appearance was adopted for the Egyptian deity Serapis, a healer of the sick and a miracle worker. His distinctive attribute was the *modius* (grain measure), an emblem of fertility, that he wore on his head (Fig. 38).

Fig 38. Serapis (left), an Egyptian deity represented in the form of a bearded Jupiter bearing a grain measure on his head, an emblem of fertility; and Juno (right), the wife of Jupiter (Fortnum B. 59, H.: 0.132m; Oldfield 60, H.: 0.142m).

Fig 39. A bronze triangular plaque of Jupiter Dolichenus in military uniform and a Phrygian cap, carrying a thunderbolt and a hammer (or axe), and standing on a bull. His wife Juno faces him (1971.26, H.: 0.17m).

Jupiter Dolichenus: The cult of Jupiter Dolichenus was similarly based in the eastern Mediterranean. Jupiter Dolichenus was the Roman interpretation of the oriental deity, Baal of Doliche (Tell Duluk in Syria). As Dolichenus, Jupiter was a god of the Universe, embracing safety, success and military triumph. Not unnaturally he was especially popular among soldiers, and evidence of his worship — cult statues, statuettes, dedications, temples, as well as triangular plaques — is widespread throughout the northern frontier regions in Britain, Germany and the Danubian provinces. A fragment of a bronze plaque in the Ashmolean shows him with his consort (Fig. 39). Jupiter wears military uniform and a Phrygian cap: he carries a thunderbolt and a hammer (or axe), and stands on a bull. His Juno faces him across a flaming altar, standing on a calf or hind: she holds a mirror.

Minerva: Minerva was an Italian goddess of handicrafts, but the Greek cult of Athena continued in its traditional forms in the Eastern Mediterranean in Roman times, as did those of most Greek analogues of Roman deities. The Ashmolean possesses a silver votive plaque to Athena (Fig. 40), who stands within a rudimentary niche holding a spear in one hand, and an owl in the other. Two gorgons' heads are stamped beneath. This plaque is said to come from Ephesus; if so, it provides an example of the products of the silversmiths who organised riots during St. Paul's visit to the city and whose slogan was "Great is Diana of the Ephesians!"

Fig 40. A Roman silver votive plaque to Minerva. It is said to come
from Ephesus; if so, it is the kind of object made by the silversmiths
who organised riots during St. Paul's visit, and whose slogan was
"Great is Diana of the Ephesians!" (1989.552, H.: 0.08m).

Household gods:　A characteristically Roman institution was the cult of the
Lar familiaris, worshipped as a household god in a *lararium* (a small, temple-like
shrine in the atrium of the house where the head of the family poured libations in
honour of domestic deities). Typically (Fig. 41) a Lar is shown alighting, with his
clothes billowing behind him. He holds a *patera* (bowl) in one hand and a *rhyton*
(an animal's head drinking horn) in the other. The *Penates* were the guardians of
the domestic foodstore. *Lares et Penates* was the Roman equivalent of "hearth and
home".

Hercules:　Hercules, the romanized Heracles, was worshipped in many
places throughout the Roman empire. One of the most outstanding Roman
objects in the Ashmolean is a marble statuette of Hercules with bow, arrows and
a club standing next to his slaughtered quarry, a boar (Fig. 42). It is a second
century AD copy of a Greek bronze statue (perhaps a work of the sculptor
Myron) of the fifth century BC. The cult of Hercules was especially popular with
merchants, as was that of Mercury. Silvanus was the Roman god of the
uncultivated part of the countryside and is often shown carrying a club
reminiscent of that of Hercules.

Fig 41. A Roman bronze statuette of an alighting Lar, a deity worshipped as a household god. *Lares et Penates* was the Roman equivalent of "hearth and home" (1970.1065, H.: 0.215m).

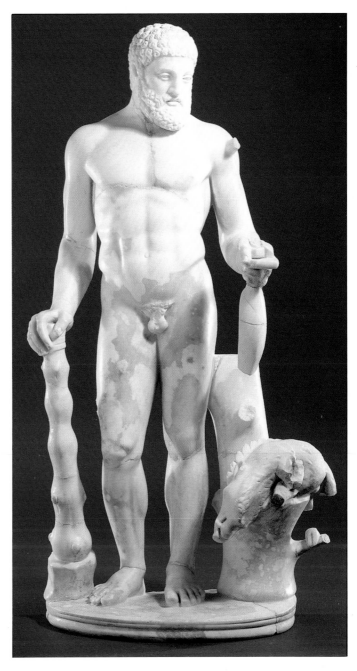

Fig 42 Roman marble statuette of Hercules with bow, arrows and a club standing next to his slaughtered quarry, a boar. It is a copy of a Greek bronze statue of the fifth century BC (1928.529, H.: 0.53m)

Fig 43. A Roman bronze statuette of Vulcan, the smith- or fire-god, found at Richborough, Kent. He wears his distinctive attribute, a pointed felt cap (1982.1121, H.: 0.105m).

Fig 44. A bronze brooch from Ostia showing Mithras kneeling on a bull he is about to slay. The cult of Mithras had its origins in Persia, and appealed to soldiers and merchants who believed it would provide immortality beyond the grave (1927.187, D.: 0.07m).

Vulcan and other gods: Vulcan was the smith- or fire-god and was especially venerated at Ostia, the port of Rome. A fine statuette was found at Richborough, Kent in 1982, and is now in Oxford (Fig. 43). Most Romano-British representations of Vulcan show him dressed in a tunic, standing with hammer and tongs at an anvil. The pose of the new statuette, naked and seated, echoes an Eastern coin type of the second to third centuries AD. An identification with Vulcan is confirmed by the felt cap on his head: naked or clothed this is Vulcan's usual attribute.

A bronze tablet in Oxford records the dedication of a lamp to Bellona, the Roman war goddess, on 15 June AD 11. The dedicant was a certain Tricunda, a slave described as a bailiff to Tiberius. The place of dedication was a township of the Ligures Baebiani, a people who had been transplanted in 180 BC from the Carrara mountains to Samnium, a mountainous region to the east of Naples, where the tablet was found.

The cults of Sol (Sun) and Luna (Moon) were assimilated with those of Apollo and Diana: they appear together on a terracotta lamp in Oxford. A moon emblem appears on a brow of a small silver gilt Diana also in the Ashmolean. The popularity of Bacchic mysteries is reflected in images of Bacchus and Ariadne, and of Silenus.

Mithras and other oriental cults: The cult of the Persian bull-slaying deity Mithras appealed to soldiers and merchants who believed that membership would provide immortality beyond the grave. Mithras slaying the bull appears in a cleverly engraved scene on a bronze brooch from Ostia and now in Oxford (Fig. 44). Mithras kneels on the bull. He has just pulled out the dagger and the dog runs forward to lick the blood. A snake creeps across the ground; a scorpion (an emblem of evil) gropes towards the bull's vitals. Mithras looks up, backwards towards the raven perched on his billowing cape. Cautes and Cautopates, the torch bearers, are represented by birds. A cock, herald of the day, represents the raised torch of Cautes; a nightingale with its evening song, the lowered torch of Cautopates.

A miniature votive hand in the Ashmolean used as a dedication in the mysteries of the cult of Sabazius, the Phrygian Jupiter, gives an insight into the wierd and wonderful aspect of Roman religion. Such votive hands were covered with cult symbols, heads of deities and signs intended to keep evil spirits at bay. The Oxford hand is so small that few of these are identifiable, but a snake can be seen slithering round the wrist and up the thumb, and a lizard crawling up the back of the hand. It is raised in the liturgical sign of benediction, a custom probably taken from the ritual of Semitic temples. The initiates of the Sabazius cult believed that after death their Good Angel would lead them to the eternal banquet — a feast anticipated on earth by means of sacred meals.

Another oriental deity is the three-bodied Artemis, a marble statuette of whom comes from the sanctuary of Men Askaenos, Kara Küyük, near Antioch in Pisidia. The goddess appears draped and hooded, and carrying a hawk in each hand. Reliefs of Cybele were also found at the same sanctuary. She is represented in Oxford by reliefs and a lamp which show her, the Great Mother goddess, enthroned, flanked by lions. She wears a mural crown and carries a *patera* (bowl) and a *tympanum* (tambourine). An even more exotic index of the degree to which cults in antiquity might be conflated is a Roman period Egyptian bronze jar or *situla* from Ephesus inscribed with hieroglyphics (Fig. 45). These record its dedication to Isis by "Padea'khonsu, musician and guard, and the son of Werer (?), mistress of the house". Isis was identified with Diana, and the two deities were honoured together at Ephesus. The cult of Asclepius — the health god — and of his daughter Hygeia, was introduced to Rome during an outbreak of plague in

Fig 45. A Roman period Egyptian bronze jar (*situla*) dedicated to Isis but found in the shrine of Diana at Ephesus, attests to the degree to which cults might be conflated in antiquity (1884.362, H.:0.12m)

Fig 46. A Roman terracotta statuette which, it has been suggested, may represent a Christian priest preaching. In the 4th century, Christianity became the *de facto* religion of the Roman empire (1910.721, H.: 0.136m).

Fig 47. A bronze statuette of a native deity from the Romano-Celtic shrine at Woodeaton, Oxfordshire; one of many votive offerings found on the site (H.: 0.06m).

Fig 48. An iron torch-holder from Woodeaton. It would have been stuck into a pole, and have carried a lump of burning pitch on its central upper projection (1952.581, H.: 0.25m).

292 BC. Their symbol was a snake, regarded by the ancients as a bringer of good health. Marble statues of both can be seen in the Ashmolean.

Judaism and Christianity: Gods might be venerated by the sacrifice of animals or the burning of incense heaped on an altar with an ornamental shovel, such as the one preserved in the Oxford collection. Animal sacrifice ceased to be practiced by the Jews after the destruction of the Temple at Jerusalem by Titus in AD 70 (when the Menorah [to be seen on lamps and a gravestone in the Ashmolean] was taken away as booty to Rome). Christians too rejected animal sacrifice, and despite prosecution, gradually increased their influence in Roman society. In AD 325, under the emperor Constantine, Christianity became the *de facto* religion of the empire, and pagan temples were deprived of their wealth. According to legend, a vision of the Christogram (the *chi-rho* symbol representing [in Greek] the first two letters of Christ's name, again to be seen on lamps in the Ashmolean) encouraged Constantine to victory at the Battle of the Milvian Bridge in AD 312. A terracotta statuette (Fig. 46) may represent a Christian priest preaching.

Romano-Celtic religion: Less than ten kilometres from the Ashmolean lies Woodeaton, the site of a Romano-Celtic shrine which flourished between the first century AD and the end of pagan antiquity in the fourth century. The temple stood within a walled enclosure on a hill overlooking the River Cherwell near the Roman road from Dorchester to Alchester. In plan, the temple corresponds to a type known as Romano-Celtic found especially in Gaul and southern Britain; such structures are very different in appearance from the ''classical'' temples of the Mediterranean in that they consist of a

Fig 49. The Felix Gem shows Ulysses and Diomede seizing an image of Athena from Troy. Made in the first century AD by the gem cutter Felix whose signature it bears, it was well known in the Renaissance, when it was used as a model by Andrea Mantegna (1966.1808, H.: 0.026m; here greatly enlarged).

central square building with a porch or verandah all round. Excavations at Woodeaton in the 1950s revealed a series of hearths inside the temple. Many votive offerings have been discovered on the site, including bronze figures of Venus and of a native goddess (Fig.47); but there is no definite evidence to identify the deity honoured at the shrine. Many of the large numbers of metal objects — bracelets and rings, brooches and fibulae, figurines of birds, amulets, inscribed plaques, model axes, coins impressed on bronze foil — were found near the gateway, suggesting that there were stalls selling offerings and souvenirs like those at many religious shrines today. It is possible that many of the bronze objects were manufactured on the spot; there is evidence for metalworking (unworked iron, bronze ingots, bronze casting waste, and slag) in the vicinity of the shrine, and many objects are of poor quality suitable only as inexpensive offerings. An unusual object is an iron torch-holder (Fig. 48) which would have been stuck into a pole, and carried a lump of burning pitch on its upper projection.

6. Food and Drink

Romans usually ate three meals a day. A light breakfast (*ientaculum*) of a little bread and fruit was taken at dawn. The midday meal (*prandium*) of fish, eggs, cold meats, vegetables and bread also tended to be light. At dinner (*cena*) many courses — some of them quite extravagant — might be consumed, the number of dishes and degree of elaboration depending on the financial resources of the host. Although a wide range of exotic foodstuffs were available, two staples of the modern kitchen — the tomato and the potato — were lacking (they were introduced from America much more recently). Tea and coffee were also absent, as was sugar. The regular sweeteners were honey and boiled (reduced) wine. Wine and (in more northerly climes) beer were the regular beverages.

A dinner party: The poet Martial, writing in the first century AD, describes a dinner for seven in terms which are not altogether exaggerated: "Stella, Nepos, Canius, Cerialis, Flaccus — will you come? My dining couch holds seven — there are six of us — add Lupus. The housekeeper from my farm has brought me digestive mallows and the various resources the garden affords, amongst which are lettuce which sits close to the ground and leeks for cutting. Burping mint will not be absent nor the aphrodisiac herb. Sliced eggs will crown a dish of Spanish mackerel with rue and there will be a moist belly of tuna from the salting barrel. These are the hors d'oeuvres. This little dinner will consist of a single course: a kid snatched from the mouth of a savage wolf, chops which do not need the carver's knife, the workman's broad beans and unsophisticated shoots. To these will be added a chicken and a ham which has already survived three dinners. When you have had enough I will give you mellow apples, wine which was three years old in Frontinus' second consulship, decanted into a Numantian flagon. In addition there will be jokes without bile, a freedom not to fear the next morning and nothing you would wish unsaid. My guests talk of chariot racing teams and our cups do not put anyone in court."

Luxury: Petronius' description of Trimalchio's feast should be consulted by anyone requiring further information about the luxury of some Roman dinners. Another source is Apicius' cookery book *De re Coquinaria*, which preserves many Roman recipes of varying degrees of complication. The Roman practice of eating dormice dipped in honey is well known; flamingoes were another occasional item at a Roman banquet; their tongues were especially prized by gourmands. Apicius gives the following instructions for cooking the complete bird: "Free the flamingo of its feathers. Wash, dress, and put it in a pan. Add water, salt, aniseed, and a little vinegar. When the bird is half cooked, bind a bouquet of chives and coriander and cook (with the flamingo). Before the bird is fully cooked, pour boiled wine over it for colouring. [To make the sauce] put into a mortar, pepper,

Fig 50. Two views of a Roman bronze saucepan. It was cast and bears the mark of the maker Nigellius, active probably in the first or second centuries A.D. The underside, as often, was cut on a lathe with elaborately turned grooves (1932.163, L.: 0.377m).

cumin, coriander, laser root, mint and rue. Bruise [these seasonings together], pour vinegar [over them], and add some dates and gravy from the pan. Empty the contents of the mortar into the same pan [with the flamingo]. Thicken the sauce with starch and pour it over the bird. Serve. The same method is used for parrot."

Saucepans: The cooking vessels of the very rich in the Roman world might be of silver. There are several saucepans of bronze in Oxford. They were originally tinned on the inside to avoid the taint of verdigris. A large pan is cast and bears the mark of the maker Nigellius who was active probably in the first or second centuries AD. The underside, as often, was cut on a lathe with elaborately turned grooves (Fig. 50). Such pans would rest on an iron trivet over an open charcoal range. Many Roman kitchens have been preserved at Pompeii and Herculaneum; a reconstructed and furnished example can be seen in the Archaeological Park at Xanten (Colonia Ulpia Traiana) in the Lower Rhine.

Al's Deli: Food shops, including fast-food establishments have also been found in these places. There is in Oxford the tombstone of a delicatessen owner of the third or fourth century AD (Fig. 51), which reads: "Alexander, sausage-seller (*butularius*) in the market (*macellum*), who lived 30 years, a good soul and the friend of all". Alexander was a member of the Jewish community at Rome, for there is a Menorah carved at the bottom of the slab.

Fig 51. The gravestone of "Alexander, sausage-seller (*butularius*) in the market (*macellum*), who lived 30 years, a good soul and the friend of all". The Menorah carved at the bottom of the slab indicates that Alexander was a member of the Jewish community at Rome (Pusey House Loan, D.: 0.32m).

Grinding: Grain was usually ground when flour was required. Bakeries at Pompeii, and presumably in many other places as well, were regularly equipped with their own mill rooms containing stone mills. The grain would be poured in the top and the upper stone turned in capstan fashion causing the grain to be ground against a stationary conical stone beneath. The flour would fall on to the platform below and be ready for use. A millstone in Oxford comes from the lower part of a smaller quern, perhaps used for milling spices. Mortaria were large mixing bowls used in Roman times for grinding and crushing food. The inside is often covered with rough grits to aid the grinding process. Sandford, Oxfordshire was a major production centre for mortaria for southern Britain in the third and fourth centuries AD.

Oil: Olive oil was a commodity of major importance in the Roman world. Not only was it used for cooking, but it was one of the principal sources of artificial light, and formed the basis of most soaps and unguents. It has been estimated that as much as a billion litres may have been required each year. By the second century AD the primary production centre was in Tripolitania (western Libya), and the local inhabitants became immensely rich as a consequence. The impressive ruins of Lepcis Magna remain as the visible sign of their wealth.

Fig 52. Samian ware from a ship wrecked on Pudding Pan Rock off the coast of Kent. Seaborne trade in ceramics at all periods of antiquity was "parasitic" on trade in more profitable items, usually foodstuffs (R. 332-3, 1909.1156-60, 1910.1-4, 1912.58, 1920.229, 1925.630, 1938.362, 1961.254-5, D. of largest pot: 0.245m).

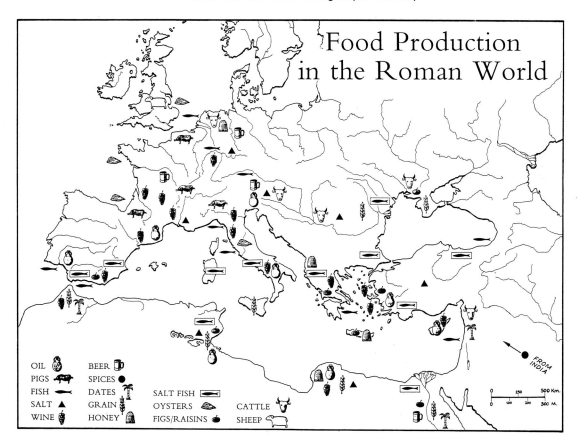

Fig 53. Staple foodstuffs, oil and wine, were shipped long distances to major urban centres in the Roman empire (after Gerlach).

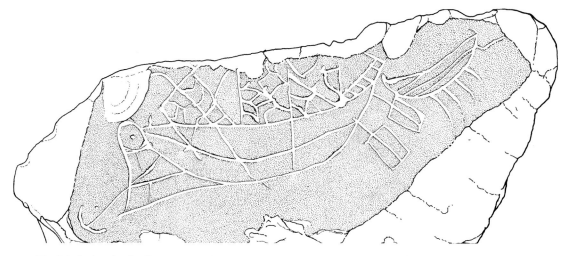

Fig 54. A sketch of a Roman merchantman carved on the marble step of a building in Utica, near Carthage in present-day Tunisia. The ship is equipped with rudders, is riding at anchor, and has a small boat attached behind (1934.72, greatest dimension: 0.22m).

Shipping: Foodstuffs might be shipped in crates, sacks, leather wineskins, or pottery amphoras. Of these, only amphoras are not biodegradable, and the archaeological record is inevitably skewed as a consequence. The insides of amphoras were regularly lined with pitch to prevent the contents seeping away through the porous pottery. Very many have been found in wrecks in the Mediterranean, the Black Sea, and the Atlantic, attesting to the fact, confirmed by surveys and excavations on land, that staple foodstuffs, grain, oil and wine, were often shipped long distances to major urban centres (Fig. 53). Another favourite item which was shipped in amphoras was *garum*, a savoury sauce made from fermented fish waste and brine — a kind of ancient anchovy relish. A mysterious commodity was silphium, a plant grown in antiquity in Cyrenaica (eastern Libya), but now extinct, widely exported and noted for its strong flavour and medicinal properties. Also from North Africa, but now in Oxford, is a sketch of a Roman merchantman (Fig. 54) carved on a marble step of a building in Utica, near Carthage in present-day Tunisia. The ship is equipped with rudders, is riding at anchor, and has a small boat attached behind.

At some time during the second half of the second century AD, a ship was wrecked on a sand bank known as Pudding Pan Rock just off the Kentish coast north of Whitstable. Most of its cargo has long perished; all that survived were some "Samian" pottery vessels from Lezoux in Central Gaul, of which pieces have been salvaged over the years (Fig. 52). This discovery reminds us that seaborne trade in ceramics at all periods of antiquity was "parasitic" on trade in more profitable items, usually foodstuffs.

7. The Army

Without an army, the Romans would never have become masters of Latium (their immediate area; *cf.* the modern Lazio), of Central Italy, of Italy as a whole, of the east and west Mediterranean, of northwest Europe south of the Rhine, or of Britain beyond the Channel. Before the first century BC, the Roman army was raised from the citizen yeomanry. By the time of the Roman emperors (from 31 BC, the beginning of the reign of Augustus), a standing professional army had been created. This consisted of legionaries — crack troops raised from among the citizen body — stationed for the most part on the frontiers of the empire. Successful soldiers were honoured with decorations, such as the silver phalerae found in the nineteenth century at Lauersfort on the Rhine, and of which the Ashmolean possesses copies. Military tombstones assist us in envisaging how these roundels adorned with the heads of deities in high relief might be arranged on the chest of a brave Roman.

There were also auxiliary troops with specialist capabilities (e.g. cavalry units, slingthrowers, sappers), who were recruited in the provinces. Twenty-five years' service in a Roman auxiliary unit was a qualification for full Roman citizenship. Discharge certificates exist which are in turn copies of imperial edicts which were set up on a wall behind the Temple of Divus Augustus in the Roman Forum. They consist of pairs of bronze tablets which list service details and bear the names of seven witnesses who vouch for the authenticity of the document.

Many military sites have been excavated, and evidence in the form of tile-stamps attests to the impressively efficient way in which the Roman army was organised. The Ashmolean collection includes military brick-stamps from opposite ends of the Roman empire. Some were found at Jerusalem and bear stamps of the Tenth Legion *Fretensis*. This legion was stationed in Jerusalem from the time of the suppression of the Jewish Revolt in AD 69 until at least AD 250. The Twentieth Legion *Valeria Victrix* was stationed at Deva, the modern Chester, from *c.* AD 88 until the mid-third century. Excavations at Holt in Denbighshire, a few kilometres up the River Dee, have uncovered a legionary works-depot which included a barrack block, a bath building and an overseer's house, as well as workshops for pottery, bricks and tiles, a drying shed and kilns. Bricks bearing the stamp of the Twentieth Legion were found at Holt; others comes from the Roman city walls of Chester. Carpow in Scotland, where the Romans were active for a limited period in the early third century AD, was probably built for part of the Sixth Legion *Victrix Britannica Pia Fidelis*, for many of their brick- and tile-stamps were found there. Even the flue tiles used to conduct hot air within the walls of the hot room of a military

bath house might be stamped, presumably to prevent illicit use elsewhere. An example in Oxford (Fig. 55) bears the stamp of the Twenty-second Legion *Primigenia Pia Fidelis*, a legion which was stationed near Mainz during the first and second centuries AD.

Sometimes military sites were only occupied for a short time. This was the case with the legionary fortress at Inchtuthil in Perthshire, begun in AD 83 by the Roman governor Agricola during his campaign in North Britain. It was an impressively large structure, 450 metres square, equipped with barrack blocks, granaries, a hospital and a headquarters' building. But everything was methodically demolished in about AD 87 after a very short period of occupation. The site was excavated in the 1960s, and one of the most striking finds was a hoard of one million nails of all sizes and types buried in a pit in order to prevent them from falling to the hands of the enemy. The excavator, the late Sir Ian Richmond, helped to finance the excavation by selling nails to visitors; some (Fig. 56) he gave to the Ashmolean.

Fig 55. Flue tiles used to conduct hot air within the walls of the hot room of a military bath house stamped with the name of the Twenty-second Legion Primigenia Pia Fidelis, stationed on the Rhine near Mainz during the first and second centuries AD (1939.120, H.: 0.356m).

Fig 56. A few of the one million nails found during the excavation of an Agricolan legionary fortress at Inchtuthil in Perthshire, a site that was occupied for a very short time before it was methodically demolished (1962.377-81, L. of longest nail: 0.26m).

8. Medicine

The medical profession was highly regarded in Roman antiquity, as is shown by the fact that practitioners were granted various privileges and immunities (such as exemption from taxation, or compulsory public services). Doctors were almost always Greeks — as, for example, Claudius Agathemerus, whose tombstone set up in Rome (Fig. 57) bears a Greek inscription: "Here lie I, Claudius Agathemerus, a doctor widely known as a swift healer of disease; this monument brings together with me my consort Myrtale; we are with the blessed in Elysium.The physician wears a toga, and his wife has a high curled wig characteristic of hairstyles of the second half of the first century and the beginning of the second century AD.

Medical practitioners were not registered, and there was much charlatanry and superstition. Pliny records in all seriousness that spittle was effective against snakes and epilepsy, and that witchcraft could be repelled by meeting

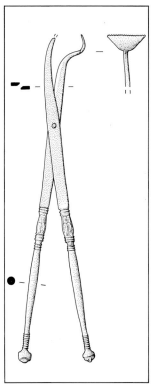

Fig 57. The tombstone set up in Rome of Claudius Agathemerus and his wife. It is inscribed in Greek: "Here lie I, Claudius Agathemerus, a doctor widely known as a swift healer of disease; this monument brings together with me my consort Myrtale; we are with the blessed in Elysium" (Michaelis 155, H.: 0.83m).

Fig 58. One of the pieces from a Roman surgeon's *instrumentarium* which includes thirty-seven objects in all. (1990.22, L. 0.212m).

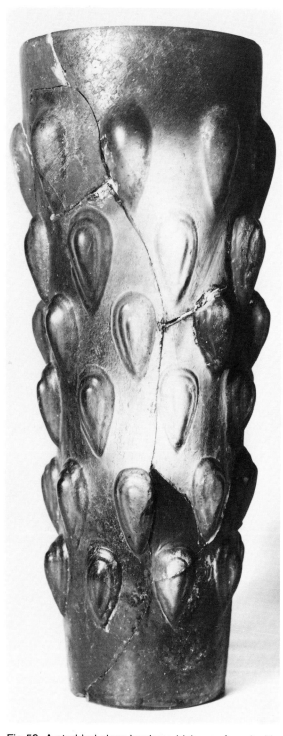

Fig 59. A studded glass beaker which was found with a set of bronze surgical instruments in a tomb near Colophon in Asia Minor (1953.636, H. 0.26m).

a person lame in the right leg. There was a high standard of medical care in the army. Legionary fortresses were equipped with *valetudinaria* (field hospitals: an impressive one was found at Inchtuthil), and skilled personnel such as surgeons and oculists bore the rank of a centurion. Surgical instruments are occasionally found in tombs, not so much perhaps for use in the next world, as to prevent them falling into unauthorized hands.

A glass vessel in Oxford (Fig. 59) was found containing a set of bronze surgical instruments in a tomb near Colophon in Asia Minor. These instruments are now in Baltimore, but another, relatively complete surgeon's *instrumentarium* is in Oxford. It numbers 37 pieces and includes a range of basic surgical tools as well as several specialised instruments. Noteworthy among these are a set of cross-legged forceps with long handles and finely cut, interlocking teeth (Fig. 58) which was used to perform a curious operation whereby the uvula — the small appendage at the back of the throat — was amputated; it may also have been used to remove haemorrhoids. The set also includes pharmaceutical equipment, and traces of medical substances have been detected in two containers. The set was probably buried in the fourth century AD, but some of the instruments may have been made long before that time.

9. Death

Burial practices varied greatly in different parts of the Roman world. At Rome itself in the early imperial period, cremation on a funeral pyre was the regular means of disposing of the dead. The ashes would be placed in an urn and deposited in a family tomb. The niches in the walls of such tombs resembled pigeon holes — to such an extent that they came to be called *columbaria*, or "dove-cotes". Many elegantly carved marble urns have survived, and some are in Oxford.

A major disadvantage of cremation in antiquity was that it used up great amounts of timber, frequently expensive perfumed timber. This was material that was also required for other purposes such as cooking, heating, shipbuilding or architectural construction. In view of this, burial in large stone coffins known as *sarcophagi* (literally "flesh-eaters") became common instead from the reign of Hadrian (AD 117-138) onwards. Sarcophagi were originally gilded and painted, and they provided a means of retaining the splendour of a traditional funeral, but at a comparatively lower cost. Many surviving sarcophagi are of marble, and are decorated with mythological scenes which presumably bore some relation to beliefs concerning the after life, though it is often difficult to find the connection. One of the finest sarcophagus reliefs in Oxford (Fig. 60) comes from the neighbourhood of Naples, and is carved with a scene of Meleager hunting the boar of Calydon. According to Greek legend,

Fig 60. The front of a Roman sarcophagus from near Naples, carved with a scene of Meleager hunting the boar of Calydon, sent by Diana (who exits on the left) as punishment for a neglected sacrifice (1947.278, H.: 0.85m).

Fig 61. Roman gold jewellery: a necklace (1932.945, L. of chain of necklace: 0.40m), earrings (1948.115, 1942.171) and finger rings (Fortnum 179, Fortnum 246, no number, Fortnum 283, 1962.434). Most extant jewellery comes from graves. The dead were often buried dressed in their finery.

Fig 62. A Roman bronze bowl and glass vessels of similar form. Neither commodity was especially expensive (but glass was the cheaper) which is probably why so many glass vessels are to be found in Roman graves (1991.12, D.: 0.218m; 1956.1016, D.: 0.165m; 1952.217, D.0.127m; 1956.1016, D.: 0.165m).

the goddess Diana was affronted on account of a neglected sacrifice and sent the boar to ravage the lands of king Oeneus. The hero Meleager was sent to confront the beast. He is shown on the sarcophagus accompanied by Atalante attacking the boar in its den. An astounded Diana rushes to the left.

At Jericho in Judaea, on the west bank of the River Jordan, several Roman period tombs were excavated by the late Dame Kathleen Kenyon on behalf of the British School of Archaeology at Jerusalem during the 1950s. Tomb K 23 was rock-cut, and fronted by an open courtyard. Inside, a central well-area was bordered on the east by a box-like hollow and a ledge running towards two *loculi* (spaces for the reception of bodies) at the far end; the west side could not be excavated.

The contents of Jericho Tomb K 23 had been completely disturbed, probably due to robbing in antiquity; and the broken and scattered objects could not be assigned to any particular burial. The remains of thirty skulls, but of few long bones suggest that over the years there had been a succession of burials with earlier bones removed and placed in ossuaries, of which one specimen, decorated with compass-drawn rosettes and zig-zag bands, is in the Ashmolean (Fig. 63). The practice of collecting bones into ossuaries began in the second half of the first century BC, and judging from the number of finds, it seems to have been particularly popular throughout the second century AD.

Fig 63. A Roman limestone ossuary from the Tomb K 23 at Jericho, decorated with compass-drawn rosettes and zig-zag bands. The practice of collecting bones into ossuaries lasted from the second half of the first century BC to the end of the second century AD (1955.552, H.: 0.26m)

Fig 64. Objects from a cremation burial from Dorchester-on-Thames, Oxfordshire. The glass vessels belong to the first half of the third century AD. The jar was already old when buried -- a hole, worn in the side by constant tipping, had been patched with lead (1886.28-30, H. of large pot: 0.41m).

Fragments of two inscribed slabs found in the courtyard, both preserving part of the name Bassus, suggest a relationship between those remembered, as might be expected in a family tomb. One reads, in Greek, "Untimely, farewell" an expression which normally indicated the grave of a young person. The glass, pottery, ossuaries and calligraphy of the inscriptions suggest a date in the second half of the first century and the beginning of the second century AD for the use of this tomb.

Glassware was frequently used for inexpensive, but dignified, grave goods throughout the Roman empire. There are hundreds of vessels in Oxford found in Roman period graves in Syria, the Crimea, Cyprus, and northwest Europe. The invention of glass blowing in Syria shortly after the middle of the first century BC meant that glass became a regular feature of everyday life — and death. It is often claimed that glass in antiquity was a luxury commodity, but this is misleading. Its status is apparent from a Jewish text of the third century AD which discusses a man wanting to apply for public assistance: "If he formerly used golden vessels, he must sell them and use silver vessels; if he

Fig 65. Nine bronze coins, of Constantine as emperor, and Crispus as Caesar, minted between 320 and 324 AD, wrapped in linen found with a skeleton on a Romano-British cemetery at Radley, Oxfordshire (Heberden Coin Room, linen: 0.06 x 0.04m).

formerly used silver vessels, he must sell them and use bronze vessels; if he formerly used bronze vessels, he must sell them and use glass vessels". There are close parallels between some surviving bronze vessels and glassware (Fig. 62). Even elaborately cut layered and caged glass was made as a cheaper version of vessels made from hard, semi-precious stone, and was placed in graves in lieu of truly luxurious items. The extremely flimsy character of much glass found in funerary contexts contrasts with the more robust glass found on residential and industrial sites, and suggests that much of the former was made specially for the tomb.

Very little cut glass is found in Britain. The only piece remotely in this category is the Wint Hill bowl (p. 23) made in imitation of rock crystal, but found in a residential rather than a funerary context. More typical is the cremation burial found outside the north-east corner of the walled town of Dorchester-on-Thames, Oxfordshire, which includes two glass vessels of the first half of the third century AD, and fragments of a third, and which were buried in a jar together with the bones of the deceased (Fig. 64). The jar was already old when buried — a hole, worn in the side by constant tipping, had been patched with lead.

Sometimes the dead were given money for their journey to the next world, but rarely in large denominations. Nine bronze coins, of Constantine as emperor, and Crispus as Caesar, minted between 320 and 324 AD, wrapped in

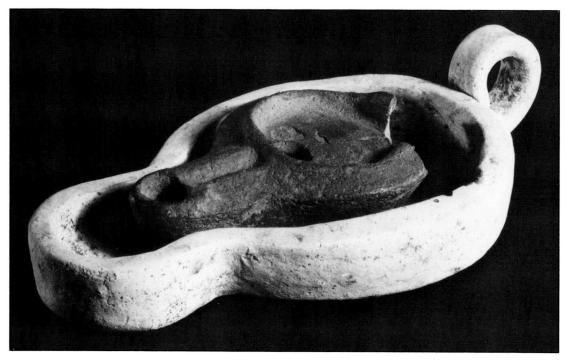

Fig 66. Roman terracotta "factory" lamp and holder found in the River Thames. Most Roman lamps, however, come from funerary contexts (1968.1175, L. 0.078m; 1948.56, L. 0.145m).

Fig 67. A Roman terracotta lamp with a relief of the story of Ulysses escaping from the Cyclops Polyphemus by hiding beneath a ram (1956.933, L. 0.105m).

Fig 68. A Roman terracotta lamp with a view of a harbour. In the background a lighthouse is being lit; in the foreground are two fishermen (1872.1324, L.: 0.153m).

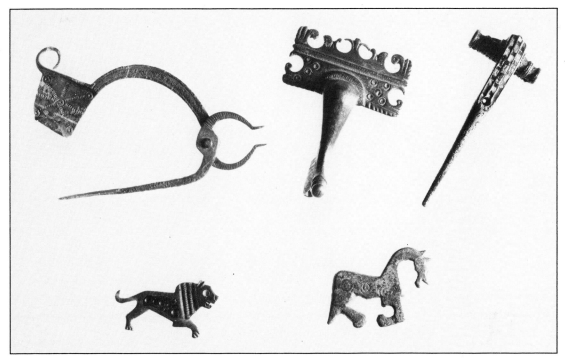

Fig 69. Roman bronze brooches from cemeteries in different parts of the northern empire: (above) a "pincer brooch" from Austria (1927.1926, L.: 0.102m), a "knee brooch" from Hungary (1891.698, H.: 0.072m), an enamelled brooch of the "head stud type" from Britain (1950.222, L.: 0.085m), (below) an enamelled lion brooch from France (1927.409, L.: 0.045m), and a horse brooch from Germany (1927.436, L. 0.044).

linen were found with a skeleton on a Romano-British cemetery at Radley, Oxfordshire (Fig. 65). While grave goods as such tended to be inexpensive, the dead were often buried wearing fine clothing fastened with brooches and fibulae. Most surviving examples are only of bronze, though some are of silver or gold. Even semi-precious stones are rarely found, but many brooches are embellished with multi-coloured glass inlays. Types of brooches vary greatly, and are frequently used by archaeologists as chronological and regional markers. The Ashmolean has rich holdings of such objects, especially brooches from Hungary, Germany, France and Britain (Fig. 61).

Terracotta lamps are another category of artefact frequently found in tombs, though they must have been widely used in life as well (e.g. the lamp and holder [Fig. 66] found — separately — in the River Thames in the nineteenth century). Dozens at a time have been found in rock-cut tombs in Israel, where they appear to have been lit to illuminate the last stages of funeral rites. Clay lamps possessed no intrinsic value, and so could be discarded without further ado. They are of interest to us, however, in that they often bear images which help to throw light — in a different sense — on the world of the Romans. They remind us that the story of Ulysses escaping from the Cyclops Polyphemus by hiding beneath a ram (Fig. 67) was as well known then as now; sometimes they provide us with townscapes (Fig. 68) which have in reality long since disappeared, and sometimes they show heavily armed gladiators fighting in the amphitheatre. These are but a few of the vast number of themes shown on Roman lamps, just as this booklet has been able to touch upon but a few aspects of a society which was in many ways as varied and complex as any before the nineteenth century.

CHRONOLOGICAL TABLE

BC	753	Legendary founding of Rome by Romulus
	c.616-509	Rome is ruled by Etruscan kings
	509	The foundation of the Roman Republic
	493	Rome joins the Latin League
	396	Rome annexes new territory
	390	The sack of Rome by the Gauls
	340-338	Rome defeats and dissolves the Latin League
	c.290	Victory over the Samnites completes Rome's domination of central Italy
	275	Rome is the undisputed ruler of southern Italy
	264-241	The First Punic War sees Rome ultimately victorious
	218-201	The Second Punic War ends in Roman victory despite Hannibal's invasion of Italy
	197	Rome defeats Philip V of Macedon
	149	Rome defeats and destroys Carthage
	146	Destruction of Corinth
	133-122	Land reforms of the brothers Gracchi
	121	Rome conquers southern Gaul
	112-106	War with the North African king Jugurtha
	81	Dictatorship of Sulla
	73-71	Slave revolt under Spartacus
	63	Consulship of Cicero
	60	Formation of the First Triumvirate: Pompey, Caesar and Crassus
	58-51	Caesar's campaigns in Gaul
	49-48	The outbreak of the Civil Wars: Caesar defeats Pompey
	48	Caesar meets Cleopatra
	46	Caesar appointed dictator for 10 years
	44	The assassination of Caesar on the Ides of March. Mark Antony takes command in Rome
	43	Octavian, Caesar's heir, is elected consul, and forms the Second Triumvirate with Antony and Lepidus
	42	The Second Triumvirate defeats Caesar's assassins at Philippi
	41	Mark Antony meets Cleopatra in Egypt
	31	Antony and Cleopatra are defeated at Actium by Octavian
	27	Octavian becomes emperor and assumes the title of Augustus
	c. 4	The birth of Christ
AD	14	Augustus dies. Tiberius becomes emperor
	37	Caligula becomes emperor
	43	The conquest of Britain is begun under Claudius
	54	Nero is emperor
	64	Rome burns, giving Nero an excuse for the first persecution of the Christians
	79	Mount Vesuvius erupts, burying Pompeii and Herculaneum
	97-117	Trajan emperor: the empire reaches its widest extent
	135	Hadrian suppresses the revolt of the Jews and denies them access to Jerusalem
	161	Marcus Aurelius is emperor
	(to 180)	Lucius Verus (Fig.70) co-emperor 161-169
	193-211	Septimius Severus is emperor
	212	Roman citizenship granted to all free inhabitants of the Roman provinces by Caracalla
	256-268	The loss and partial recovery of the Danube provinces and Syria
	273	Destruction of Palmyra
	285	Diocletian emperor
	312	Constantine wins the battle of the Milvian bridge
	330	Foundation of Constantinople
	400-476	The fall of the Roman empire in the West

A marble bust of the emperor Lucius Verus, "weak, indulgent and a poor administrator".
It was found at Probalinthus, near Marathon in Attica, and had probably been set up by the wealthy
Athenian philosopher Herodes Atticus, to whom the education of Lucius Verus and Marcus
Aurelius was entrusted. (1947.277. H.: 0.68m).

Select Bibliography

General:

A.C. Brown, *Ancient Italy Before the Romans* (Oxford, 1980)

T. Cornell and J. Matthews, *Atlas of the Roman World* (Oxford, 1982)

F.R. Cowell, *Everyday Life in Ancient Rome* (London, 1961)

S.S. Frere, *Britannia: a History of Roman Britain* 3rd edn (London, 1987)

K. Greene, *The Archaeology of the Roman Economy* (London, 1986)

R. Jenkyns, *The Legacy of Rome: a new appraisal* (London, 1992)

B. Jones and D. Mattingly, *An Atlas of Roman Britain* (Oxford, 1990)

N. Lewis and M. Reinhold, *Roman Civilization: Selected Readings* 3rd ed(New York, 1990)

F. Millar, *The Emperor in the Roman World 31BC–AD337* (London, 1977)

D. Strong and D. Brown, *Roman Crafts* (London, 1976)

M. Vickers, *Ancient Rome* (Oxford, 1990)

J. Wacher, *The Roman World* (London, 1987)

The Renaissance:

R. Weiss, *The Renaissance Discovery of Classical Antiquity* (Oxford, 1969)

Felix Gem:

M. Vickers, "The Felix Gem in Oxford and Mantegna's triumphal programme", *Gazette des Beaux-Arts* (March 1983) 97-104

Arundel Marbles:

D.E.L. Haynes, *The Arundel Marbles* (Oxford, 1975)

D. Howarth, *Lord Arundel and his Circle* (New Haven, 1985)

Pottery:

M. Vickers, J. Allan and O. Impey, *From Silver to Ceramic: the Potter's Debt to Precious Metal in the Greco-Roman, Islamic and Oriental Worlds* (Oxford, 1986)

Woodeaton:

M.V. Taylor, "Woodeaton", *Journal of Roman Studies* 7 (1917) 98- 119

J. Kirk, "Bronzes from Woodeaton, Oxon.", *Oxoniensia* 14 (1949) 1- 45, pls 1-6

R.G. Goodchild and J. Kirk, "The Romano-Celtic temple at Woodeaton", *Oxoniensia* 19 (1954) 15-37, pls 1-3

Shakenoak:

A.C.C. Brodribb, A.R. Hands and D.R. Walker, *Excavations at Shakenoak* 1-5 (Oxford, 1968-1978)

Pewter:

D. Brown, "A Roman pewter hoard from Appleford, Berks", *Oxoniensia* 38 (1973) 184-206.

Wint Hill Bowl:

D.B. Harden, "The Wint Hill hunting bowl and related glasses", *Journal of Glass Studies* 2 (1960) 45-82

Nalbinding:

R. Rutt, *A History of Hand Knitting* (London, 1987)

Food and Drink:

A. Briers, *Eat, Drink and Be Merry* (Oxford, 1990)

J. Edwards (ed.), *The Roman Cookery of Apicius Translated and Adapted for the Modern Kitchen* (London, 1988)

G. Gerlach, *Essen und Trinken in römischer Zeit* (Cologne, 1986)

Medicine:

R. Jackson, *Doctors and Diseases in the Roman Empire* (London, 1988)